That I May Fly

Poems (and the Reasons Why)

Dan McHenry Hicky
Col. USAF, Ret.

UNITED
WRITERS PRESS, INC

United Writers Press, Inc.
P.O. Box 326
Tucker, Georgia 30085-0326
www.unitedwriterspress.com
1-866-857-4678

ISBN: 0-9760824-6-2
ISBN-13: 978-0-9760824-6-0

Library of Congress Control Number: 2005930216

Printed and bound in the United States of America.

ACKNOWLEDGEMENTS

There are many to whom I owe my thanks, and I dare not try to list them lest I leave someone out. However, four special people have regularly assisted me in sustaining my poetry habit and for making this book possible, and deserve special mention: My daughter, Mina, for her proofreading and helpful suggestions; my son, Stratton, for keeping my word processor going; Monaray Powers for typing the poems in preparation for my weekly column, and Adelaide Ponder, longtime editor of the Madisonian, who talked me into doing the column in the first place.

DEDICATION

This book is dedicated to my wife, Hattie Mina, the best lover, companion and friend a man could wish for. The poems ODE TO MY WIFE and FOLLOW UP were written for one of her birthdays and, I think, make an appropriate dedication.

ODE TO MY WIFE

In this tangled web we call life
A man's whole fate may well depend
On his selection of a wife,
Who must also be his friend.

God helped me in my selection
With his knowledge, so divine.
He gave me absolute perfection
When he made Hattie Mina mine.

FOLLOW UP

In spite of this perfection,
We sometimes disagree
When choosing our direction,
One for you and one for me.

But after fifty eight years
We've really learned to cope
And avoid those bitter tears;
When you say yes, I never say nope.

So here's wishing you a happy birthday,
With many more to follow.
And if you must go your way,
I'll be sure to follow.

TABLE OF CONTENTS

INTRODUCTION

The poems in this book were selected from six years of columns in my hometown newspaper, THE MADISONIAN, and it's successor, THE MORGAN COUNTY CITIZEN. They tell the story of my military career and retirement to my home town of Madison, Georgia. Each poem is introduced with the reason why it was written. Collectively they represent a "senior citizen's" concept of poetry and my preference for poetry that rhymes.

Robert Frost, one of the most important American poets, once said, "I would as soon play tennis without a net as write free verse." I tend to agree with him. Although I am not opposed to free verse, it's just not for me at this point in time. I have read and heard beautiful readings of free or blank verse but to me it was lovely prose, not poetry. I believe that free verse is a genre unto itself and deserves a name of its own. Here's a suggestion.

PROETRY

Ever since World War Two
Free verse has been THE THING.
No longer must poems have
Rhythm and rhymes that sing.

Free verse may be beautiful
But lacking the rhythm and rhyme
That makes real true poetry
Something that is sublime.

Free verse is just glorified prose,
So what was formerly called poetry,
In a free verse form of expression,
Might now be called PROETRY.

With this free form of writing,
What was once called a poem,
Without fear of contradiction,
Could now be called a PROEM.

THAT I MAY FLY

LEAVES OF LIFE

I enlisted in the Army Air Corps December 5, 1940. My first assignment was to the Air Corps Communications School, Scott Field, Illinois. My first Christmas in the military was spent among strangers in a strange place. I was a lonely buck private with no inkling of what the future might bring. Maybe it's this kind of situation that brings out the muse of poetry. For me, that is often the case. After a lonesome Christmas Eve wandering around nearby Saint Louis, I returned to my tent at Scott Field and composed this poem.

A tree has just so many leaves,
A life just so many days.
Does a tree cling to its leaves
As we cling to our days?

Some days pass like leaves that fall
So slowly from the autumn trees
That we wonder if they move at all,
Such restless days are these.

Leaves by a gentle zephyr blown
Are so quick to reach the ground.
Dancing leaves like days we've known
And in them much joy have found.

Wintry blasts blow withered leaves,
Like heartbreak days piled high,
That bare our souls like naked trees
Against a cold and sodden sky.

Oh naked tree and barren heart,
Cling not to leaf or day,
For Shelley says "If winter come,
Spring can't be far away."

New leaves, new days, new songs to sing.
Stout heart do not despair,
For after snow come lilacs in the spring,
An answer to earth's prayer.

IDEALS

In 1941, after becoming an instructor at the Air Corps Communications school, I applied for flight training. I was sent to the Sparton School of Aeronautics in Tulsa, Oklahoma. I was the only southerner in that school. One of my classmates was named Hires, an heir to the Hires root beer fortune. The upperclassmen made me stand on the mess hall table and sing "Glory, Glory To Old Georgia" while Hires sang the Pepsi Cola song.

World War II began and I received my wings and commission in May of 1942. The graduation ceremony was a parade and formal pinning on of wings by a family member or girlfriend. None of my family nor my girlfriend could attend so my instructor pinned on my wings. I was feeling lonesome and after a lonely meal returned to the barracks. This wasn't the happy ending I had hoped for. That evening I wrote the following poem.

Ideals we should all cherish;
They start with youth and last,
Until, with time, they perish
And then become the past.

There are some who have commended
Work well done thus joy complete.
But as each task is finally ended,
What is the joy, tasks to repeat?

Others sing of bright parades,
Of happiness and love divine.
But, with time, that also fades
Like the love that once was mine.

Ideals belong to all mankind.
In life's struggle each will fight
Til at the end what does one find?
Oblivion, eternal night?

CHILL

After receiving my wings and 2nd lieutenant commission in May of 1942, I was sent to The Republic of Panama with a group of pilots to defend the canal. My squadron was stationed at a landing strip about twenty miles south of Panama City. We were deep in a tropical jungle and rarely got back to civilization. We were flying single engine P39s and P40s in hot and humid weather. On every flight I lost several pounds from perspiration. In spite of this I loved the flying.

In the summer of 1943 I developed a tropical fever. The flight surgeon confined me to the infirmary until the fever was gone. This took over a week and I was the only one there. The chills and fever had me feeling mighty low. The poem "CHILL" was written during that stay in the infirmary.

(With apologies to Edgar Allen Poe)

As I lie in fevered bed
Many thoughts run through my head,
While my pounding heart is beating
An awful voice keeps on repeating:

"Do not fear this lonely meeting"
As I ponder on this greeting,
While my heart is beating, beating,
That awful voice keeps on repeating:

"Do you wonder where you are?
This is a place so very far
That only pain can enter here,
But you are near, so very near."

By now my brain is whirling
From this scene unfurling
And as I try to break away,
That voice says "You must stay."

Now I look and see a room,
Black as night, dark as doom.
This starts my blood congealing
And sends my poor brain reeling.

For in the center, I am there
And in my eyes a vacant stare.
Nothing hearing, nothing seeing,
Can this be me, this other being?

Strangely too, the room's transparent.
Now, to my eyes, it is apparent
That there are so many others
That I tremble neath my covers.

For in each there is a being
Nothing hearing, nothing seeing.
This can be no consolation
If each has my own sensation.

And now that voice again repeating
While my heart is beating, beating
No one here is hearing, seeing
But each one is feeling, feeling.

Now I know that it is here,
The thing that I have come to fear
And all the time that voice repeating
While my heart is beating, beating:

"No one here is hearing, seeing
But each one is feeling, feeling."
While my brain is reeling, reeling
It comes upon me stealing, stealing.

Like a serpent slowly weaving
Through my body and there leaving
All her spawn, now to be fed
Upon my being in that bed.

Now, more sudden than it came,
The vision leaves, but just the same,
That awesome voice is still repeating:
"Do not fear this lonely meeting."

Now that voice is still repeating
While my heart is beating, beating:
"Pain can be so fleeting, fleeting.
Do not fear this lonely meeting."

Then I wake in perspiration
With a newborn inspiration
Never to fear that lonely meeting
That can be so fleeting, fleeting.

TO YOU, MY WIFE

After my bout with tropical fever in 1943, things began to look up. In 1944, I married Hattie Mina Reid and headed for combat. (I hasten to explain that these were two entirely separate events.)

Hattie Mina and I had known each other all our lives and had been corresponding on a regular basis. I was madly in love and had broached the subject of marriage but she would never say "yes." After trying during the whole tour in Panama, I was finally given a combat assignment along with a thirty day leave.

This could be my only chance and I was determined to get the matter settled. Hattie Mina kept me in a daze and did not say yes until we were standing before the minister in the church at the wedding ceremony. We had a short, but wonderful honeymoon in Miami Beach, as I had to catch a flight back to Panama and Hattie Mina had to return to her teaching job. I was deeply in love and missed Hattie Mina very much. It was during this period of separation, while I waited for orders assigning me to a combat squadron in Europe, that this poem was written.

I want my arms around you,
I love all the charms about you,
And how I miss that heavenly kiss,
That tells me you love me too.

The sweet scent of your hair,
The warmth when you are there,
The look in your eyes that belies
How much you've begun to care.

With the touch of your lips
The whole world flips,
While my heart shivers,
Stumbles and quivers.

My darling I'll always love you
And pray the Angels above you
Will forever be as kind to me
As the day they let me love you.

A FIGHTER PILOT'S PRAYER

During the latter part of 1944, I received orders assigning me to a fighter squadron in France to fly P47 Thunderbolt fighters. It was necessary for me to be checked out in this plane at Riverhead, Long Island. I was able to leave Panama, go by way of Madison, pick up Hattie Mina and drive to Riverhead. We, along with several other couples, stayed in a hotel in Riverhead. Most of us were newlyweds and this was like a second honeymoon. We had mixed emotions about going off to war. "A Fighter Pilot's Prayer" was written during this period.

Almighty God who made the sky,
I offer thanks that I may fly,
My wings aloft in that great space,
Which, to me, reflects thy face.

Each dawn patrol, each sunset flight,
Makes clear, to me, thy wondrous might.
So please, dear Lord, forgive my sin,
If when I fly, I fly to win.

To use these wings to shoot and kill;
That is my sin and not thy will.
So please, dear Lord, forgive my sin,
If when I fight, I fight to win.

No matter what the end might be,
My lord I give my thanks to thee,
Almighty God, who made the sky,
I offer thanks that I may fly.

CONVOY BOUND FOR WAR

*The training period at Riverhead, Long Island was hurried but
Hattie Mina and I managed to get a few days together in New York City
where the USO provided tickets to several Broadway shows. These days
ended all too soon and I had to report to Fort Dix for transportation to
Europe. I was given a berth on a troop ship, part of a large convoy. The
first day at sea I was standing by the rail watching the sunset when,
in the distance, I saw the white sail of a small fishing boat silhouetted
against the sky. The comparison between this lone small boat and the
large convoy of ships was the inspiration for this poem.*

In a fishing boat on a peaceful sea,
Neath the warmth of the blazing sun,
Sits a fisherman lost in reverie,
His day's catch almost done.

When over the horizon's rim
Appears an awesome sight,
Now so familiar to him,
In all its fearsome might.

It's a convoy bound for war
Beneath the azure sky,
With muffled engines roar
As silent ships glide by.

Spinning turbines turn
Angry propeller blades,
In waters neath the stern,
For these macabre parades.

The convoy slowly fades away,
Like the dreams we humans make,
Leaving bubbles and foamy spray
In a long dark green wake.

The sea's green takes on a golden glow
From the fiery ball of the setting sun.
Daylight fades as evening breezes blow
And the convoy continues it's run.

Ships sailing on a sunset trail
Leaving behind a wake of foam
And one small white sail
With its course set for home.

FLASHBACK

Upon reaching Europe I was rushed to a fighter squadron in France and was soon leading ground support missions over Germany. One of our assignments was to destroy enemy transportation which consisted mostly of trains. Sometimes, at the critical moment of a flight, I would have a flash of memory from the past which I called flashbacks.

Have you ever had a flashback?
Memories of things you once did?
Some things from very far back
When you were just a kid?
Even some that best stay hid?

Flashbacks come as a surprise
And they only last a moment,
But in that moment often lies
A message of great importance,
Important to that instance.

On a mission to strafe a train,
While diving down with guns ablaze,
A flashback entered my busy brain
And I recalled, as if in a daze,
Some earlier and more happy days.

The toy train of my childhood,
The locomotive was my prize,
Yet, at that very moment, I would
Destroy a train of full size.
My psyche asked, "Is this wise?"

The flashback was instantaneous
And for my mission, on that day,
Was most certainly extraneous.
I was immediately on my way,
Forgetting children's play.

As I continued the strafing runs,
Clouds of steam from a gaping hole
Made by tracers from my guns,
Told me I had fulfilled my role,
But at what cost to my eternal soul?

REFLECTIONS ON A PARTY NIGHT

When the war in Europe ended, my squadron decided to have a party. There was a sense of relief and jubilation and as such things do, the celebration became quite a blowout and we overdid it, only to suffer the consequences the next day.

Returning from an all night spree
I wondered what had become of me.
Where were the ideals I once had,
The things looked up to as a lad.

Can all this raucous gaiety
I heard on every side of me,
Be, in any way, true reality?
My soul says "This can't be."

And so I crawl into my GI bed
With strange thoughts in my head,
Wild thoughts, a sleepless night
Ravaged with a noxious blight.

While tossing on my fevered cot
My thoughts turn to trash and rot.
My mind cries out for better things
But all I hear is creaking springs.

With noisy springs I toss and turn
And all the time my soul does yearn
For love, beauty, truth and realities.
Where do you look for such as these?

Now slowly the dawn grows near
Thoughts begin to shape and clear
Love. beauty, truth and reality,
All this time have been with me.

Though dormant in my blighted mind
My soul says others were more kind.
Those who I know will always be
At home each night to pray for me.

MY CITADEL

With the war in Europe over, my squadron was ordered to return to the United States, regroup and prepare for assignment to the Pacific Theater. Our base for regrouping was at La Junta, Colorado. This was the first chance Hattie Mina and I had had to live together since our marriage. For her, La Junta was a bleak and barren landscape compared to the lush greenery of Georgia. Rental housing was scarce and not very enticing. What an introduction to married life for Hattie Mina! The war in the Pacific Theater ended and our squadron was decommissioned. A succession of three year assignments at various locations including three years in Japan followed. Hattie Mina endured all of this with beauty, charm and grace becoming MY CITADEL.

My wife is a citadel
In which all things of beauty dwell.
My refuge from monotony,
My place of sweet tranquility.

I look upon her lovely face
And am aware of every grace,
Of beauty which I never knew
Until the love between us grew.

To her I lose my every longing
In the joy of our belonging
To each other throughout life.
Oh, my citadel, my wife.

THE CASE OF THE HAPLESS HUSBAND

One of my three year assignments was at Strategic Air Command Headquarters, Omaha, Nebraska. While there Hattie Mina decided she wanted a certain kind of strapless slip for her birthday. I knew nothing about slips and could not find the kind she wanted. Poetry came to my rescue resulting in this poem.

Husbands are a sorry lot and this one oh so hapless.
Your birthday gift WOULD be a slip, and one that's strapless.
After searching allover this darn town,
In little stores and stores of great renown,
I find that slips are few
Especially one that might fit you.
So, even though the slip is missing,
A happy birthday I am wishing
And hoping that this check will do
To show how much I LOVE YOU.

COMING HOME

After assignments in Louisiana, Florida, Illinois, Japan, Alabama and Colorado, I completed thirty years of active duty and retired, returning to my hometown of Madison, Georgia. The old family home dating back to 1822 was still occupied by family. Hattie Mina and I wanted a home of our own so we bought a house and settled down in it. After a few years my mother, grandmother and aunt, who had been living in the old family home where I grew up, passed away and the old home was deserted. I decided to renovate the old house and will never forget my emotions as I entered that dark and empty house.

The place where my ancestors were born,
The family home was lonesome and forlorn.
As I entered through the front door
My mind was filled with family lore.

The old ceiling lamp in the front hall
Cast a dim somber light upon the wall.
A feeling of emptiness filled the room,
An atmosphere of darkness and gloom.

This old house had always been the place
Where many generations lived to face
Whatever fate would bring their way
As the house lived on for another day.

Turning on successive lights as I roam
Through the old house, my childhood home,
Each new light brings to my view
Many things, that as a child I knew.

As the warm light begins to spread
The gloom is gone and there instead
Is a golden glow of warmth and cheer,
A good feeling of family being near.

The house rouses from its sleep
Releasing memories from its keep,
Memories of those who lived there
Within it's tender loving care.

Now it becomes very clear to me,
The old house just wants to see
What each new generation brings
As the years pass on silent wings.

I hope that during my tenure
Some how I'll be able to insure
That this old house will always be
A home for those who follow me.

AN OLD HOUSE

When I returned to Madison in 1972, I wanted to reacquaint myself with the town. It has been my experience that the way to really see a location is to walk the whole area. I started walking around Madison and have continued to do so. My walking today is limited to a regular route because of deteriorating sight. On one of my early walks I came across an old house nearly hidden behind the untended brush and growth in the yard. It was deserted, run down and dilapidated. It appeared to have been a very nice house at one time but not occupied for a long time. It was a sad and depressing sight and I could not get it out of my mind. Sometime later while walking near the site, I discovered that the house had been torn down and removed. I hate to see old things fall to neglect and disrepair, including myself. Since I could not get the old house off my mind, I decided a poem might help.

It was an old old house in an old old town.
Its paint was peeling and it was run down;
Yet it had been home and it was still home
To the wanderer who had ceased to roam.

As he walked down the lonely street,
Wondering what he would next meet,
He felt a cold and shivering sweat,
Wondering if the house were there yet.

When he turned the corner, it was still there
Looking deserted, bleak and bare.
The house looked so neglected and old
That he felt his heart grow very cold.

Where were the people who once lived there
In this old house now so bleak and bare?
The family he had so longed to find
Who had always remained in his mind.

They were all gone, he knew not where,
Leaving this old house so bleak and bare.
Yet it had been home and it was still home
To the one who no longer wanted to roam.

MINA'S ROOM

My children spent most of their school years prior to college in Colorado Springs, Colorado. We built a home in Colorado Springs with enough room for each of our three children to have a bedroom. Since Mina, our first born, was the only girl, her room was kind of special. Her furniture was a light cream color with gold trim. After Mina married after graduation from college, we kept that furniture in her room. When we returned to Madison, the furniture came with us and is now in "Mina's room." Every time I enter that room, memories of Mina flood my mind.

The room is always ready,
But the dresser is bare
Without her cherished teddy,
And Mina is not there.

The furniture has not changed,
Every piece is still there,
Nothing has been rearranged,
But Mina is not there.

The bedspread is the same,
And so is every chair,
Just as when she last came,
But Mina is not there.

Her spirit dominates the scene,
Her perfume scent is in the air,
Just as if she could be seen,
But now, Mina is not there.

So many memories are kept here
Of a daughter, once in my care.
Her room brings her Memory near,
But now Mina is not there.

THE STREETS OF MADISON

Madison was once a small community of beautiful homes. Today, when I want to experience that atmosphere of my youth, I roam the back streets and alleys.

Madison has gained some renown
As a beautiful historic town.
Its true essence is found
By simply wandering around.

Along the main street thoroughfare
Beautiful homes once stood where
Filling stations and parking lots
Now occupy the choice spots.

Main street is a noisy traffic mess
Yet back streets retain a quaintness
In the shade of ancient tree arches
Oblivious to the way time marches.

Antebellum homes along the way
Each with something else to say.
Tales of people from long ago
And how the town began to grow.

Boxwood gardens all along the way,
Spired churches where people pray.
Iron and picket fences in profusion,
Mainly to prevent animal intrusion.

Interesting small back alleyways
Named for people of long gone days
Who constructed these great houses
For themselves and their spouses.

Winding lanes through the cemetery
Sometimes, at night, quite scary.
Shadows across the resting places
Of so many dear departed faces.

Here on Academy and Old Post Road
Many courtly gentlemen once strode.
The famous Stagecoach Inn was here
With boy's and girl's schools near.

The back streets of Madison reveal
The old town's true historic appeal.
Quaint back streets now hold the key
To this old town's glorious history.

PROGRESS IN A LITTLE TOWN

Every time I am in one of the newly developed areas of my hometown I can't help remembering the way things used to be. Some things may be better and some worse. That's a matter of opinion, but I still reminisce about the way things were when I was growing up.

The little town has grown a lot;
Where once were cotton fields
There is now a parking lot
With sun shining on windshields.

Paving now reflects the heat
From the summer mid day sun.
Fields replaced by concrete
Leave nature's work undone.

Rural scenes have been replaced
By acres of concrete and cars.
The little town has been defaced
By "Progress" and its scars.

Main street is now a thoroughfare
Where heavy streams of traffic flow,
Always moving here and there,
But never, ever, moving slow.

The downtown square is not the same.
There used to be so many stores
But since the likes of Wal-mart came
There are so many closed doors.

Yet some things have not changed,
They will always be there.
Even though the town is rearranged
God's churches are still there.

MADISON'S GHOSTS

Along with its history and charm Madison has ghosts. This poem concerns those that I know about. I'm sure there are others.

Madison is an historic town
With many beautiful old homes
And some of them are haunted
With a ghost that still roams.

In one of the stately mansions
A ghost insists on being served.
Whenever a social event occurs
She feels a drink is deserved.

This ghost, a servant girl,
Was murdered on the property.
Her spirit wants to make sure
She is remembered properly.

A drink must be left for her
Whenever there's a big party;
If not she knocks out the slats
Of the host's bed. She's a smarty.

In one beautiful columned mansion
Spirits refuse to leave this earth.
Their ghostly presence is indicated
By an image on the fireplace hearth.

Efforts to remove this eerie sign
Despite many attempts have failed.
That image remains to this day
Although it has slightly paled.

In another much lived in home
A mother's spirit lingers there.
The present occupants often hear
Her heavy footsteps on the stair.

Then there's the rocking chair
That often rocks all by itself.
Could this be a worn out ghost
Rocking in lonely silent stealth?

In this historic town of Madison
Many stories of ghosts abound
And if there be so many tales
There must be ghosts around.

THE RUMBLE OF PIPES

Pipe organs have always fascinated me with their capability of producing the deep bass notes that no other instrument can equal. Electronic organs just can't equal the sound from a big bass pipe.

Pipe organs are wondrous things,
Each one has its own personality;
Each capable of producing notes
That often seem to defy reality.

The deep bass rumble of mighty pipes
Can actually vibrate the floor
Sending tingles up and down my spine
Making me want to hear more.

The awesome rumble of a pipe organ
Can not be reproduced by electronics.
Only a real pipe organ can thunder
And shake a building with its sonics.

The smaller organs without pipes
Can't produce the thundering bass.
They just sound like accordions
Striving hard to keep up the pace.

Pipe organs have real character
Each one of them handmade,
The rumble of their unique sound
In my memory will never fade.

SENIOR MOMENTS

My wife recently gave me a hat that looks like a fisherman's hat, but different. On the front, in big letters, it says SENIOR MOMENT SURVIVOR and instead of fisherman's flies it has boxes for memory pills, a compass for finding directions and a magnifying glass for reading directions. I've been wondering if she's trying to tell me something. Anyway it gave me the idea for a poem.

A senior moment might occur
When you least expect it.
A moment to make you wish
That you could reject it.

There are memory lapses
That defy explanation.
They can be embarrassing
Causing much consternation.

You know the clock is wrong
And you set out to set it,
Just then the doorbell rings,
And you decide to get it.

The clock has been forgotten
Until you hear it chime
And you suddenly realize
That it's the wrong time.

There are even occasions,
At the refrigerator door,
When you wonder what it was
That you came there for.

Waking up in the dark,
As your feet hit the floor,
Do you wonder if it's morning
Or the night before?

When you meet an old friend,
Whose name you can't recall,
Do you begin to wonder
If memory's working at all.

These little memory lapses
Soon make you realize
You've had a senior moment
Much to your surprise.

INSUFFICIENT DATA

This generation has more information available through computers and the internet than my generation ever dreamed of. Hopefully all this information will be used wisely. As computers can be used to control most anything, if my sight was what it should be, I would be right in there with the computer generation. I often think of the human brain as the ultimate computer and look forward to the eventual union of the brain and the computer. Of course, there will always be problems.

Through a misty veil
My brain really tries
With effort to prevail
And clear clouded eyes.

I end up in despair
If I try to compensate
For this sorry affair,
Which is now my fate.

My computer, or my brain
Asks "What is the matter?
You make me really strain,
With insufficient data."

There are compensations
Provided by God's grace.
These other sensations
Can take sight's place.

Armed with this information,
It really doesn't matter.
Lacking sight's sensation,
There's still enough data.

ROCKY

When we were first stationed in Colorado, my wife, Hattie Mina, rescued a beautiful grey, long-haired Persian cat from some boys who had been chasing him. She had a grey Persian when she was growing up so Hattie Mina wanted to keep this cat. He was the typical cat demanding his privileges, privacy and regular meals. He could be very affectionate when he wanted to but he always maintained the regal air of royalty. Apparently he had been well raised and cared for. No one claimed him and he had made himself a member of the family so we kept him. He remained with us until we were transferred to an Air Force Base in Florida.

Our pet Rocky was just a cat,
But you'd better not tell him that.
He was a long haired Persian cat,
Which made him an aristocrat.

His attitude was always regal,
Yet to birds he was lethal,
While in his people's house,
There never lived a single mouse.

His tastes were most expensive,
And his needs so very expansive.
Rockafellow had to be the name,
For a cat who played that game.

Rocky was a Colorado cat,
High altitude his habitat.
Moving to Florida, not his plan,
So, along the way, he ran.

We lost Rocky along the way,
But he's remembered to this day,
And somewhere on Alabama's coast,
Someone else is Rocky's host.

MANSIONS

I usually wake up around five thirty each morning. Often it is a dream that wakes me and that dream haunts me the rest of the morning or the rest of the day. Many times these haunting dreams lead to the composition of a poem. Today's poem is one of these. At my age one's mortality comes to mind. I do not see it as a morbid subject to be avoided. To me there is some comfort in the subject and I intend to have more poems about this later.

I dreamed of many mansions
But there was none for me.
This raised many questions:
What more was there to see?

Crystal chandeliers from the ceiling
Cast their ethereal light.
It gave me an awesome feeling
To see such a wondrous sight.

I wandered through marble halls
Filled with many treasures
And on each of the walls
Were tapestries of pleasures.

Each tapestry depicted scenes
From the life of the occupant.
It was by this unusual means
That I knew his life was relevant.

"In my father's house are many mansions…"
Could there not be one for me?
Of all my many questions
This one meant the most to me.

My dream was fulfilled, indeed,
For I was made to see,
That for my little "mustard seed"
There was a modest home for me.

SHADOWS

Sometimes I take my walk in the evenng as the sun is setting and the shadows begin to form. As the street lights come on, many interesting shadow patterns are formed. Watching the various shadowy images always gets me in a thoughtful mood. This poem was the result of one of those moods.

I remember shadows when they fell,
As eventide rang the day's death knell.
Long shadows with tall tales to tell,
Short shadows, little imps from hell.

Shadows of both the good and bad,
Like memories that we've all had,
Of the good times that we cherish,
And memories better left to perish.

The memories of things long past,
Short glimpses that do not last,
Like shadows which so often cast,
Their images that fade so fast.

I wonder if the shadows know,
Of memories that come and go,
Like dark shadows in the night,
Dependent on a source of light?

Like the shadows that soon fade,
The plans that we've all made,
Are only flimsy wisps of smoke,
Escaping from routine's dull yoke.

Some memories are not always clear.
Like shadows they soon disappear,
And never leave a single trace,
To show they occupied that space.

Some lives, like shadows, leave no trace,
To indicate that they took place,
While other lives shine so bright,
No shadows can be seen in the night.

Oh that my shadow might fall,
On someone who will recall,
That my life shed some light,
To brighten up the dark night.

NIGHTMARES

Nightmares can be disturbing whether caused by something that happened during the preceding day or by overindulgence the night of the dream. Nightmares often leave lingering recollections for several days. That is what happens to me.

Nightmare dreams of demons,
Even though not real ones,
Sometimes visit me at night
And then feed upon my fright.

Demons sometimes follow me
And hide behind every tree.
But when I turn around
Those demons can't be found.

Poe's sharp pendulum swinging,
Its gleaming blade singing
As it slowly nears my head
Filling me with awesome dread.

As I dream of strange places,
There are no familiar faces.
Suddenly everything revolves
As the eerie scene dissolves.

Nightmares are passing things
Reminding us of life's stings,
Oft arriving on midnight wings,
Departing as the Angelus rings.

BAD NIGHT

Have you ever had a bad night when sleep would not want to come and when it did it was nightmarish? After eating unwisely one evening, I had a bad night like that. It was disconcerting. To clear my mind I put the experience in verse.

Have you waked in the night,
With a strange premonition,
A feeling of sudden fright
Concerning your condition?

You seem to have the feeling,
That something's watching you.
An uneasy, squeamish feeling,
One entirely new to you.

What will this night bring?
Apparently nothing is there.
But is something frightening
At the bottom of the stair?

There's only one solution:
Get up and look around.
What if your constitution
Can't stand what is found?

As I weigh the possibilities
And am wondering what to do,
The world's normal activities
Continue as dawn breaks through.

My premonition soon disappears
And I begin to realize
That all my silly quaking fears
Came from too many French Fries.

MY CANDLE

My poetry often seems to have a life of its own, taking me into new dimensions. This poem, about a sleepless night, contains metaphors and allegory. I wonder if you can tell what it is really about...

One dark and stormy night
There was no power or light.
A lone candle let me see
And brought about this reverie.

My candle burned so bright
Yet it cast a mellow light.
It was such a pretty sight
I wanted it to last the night.

Its flickering yellow light
Formed shadows on the wall.
It was an enchanting sight,
Those images I recall.

Myriad shapes and forms
Dancing there in my room
While the weather stormed
Mid many a thunderous boom.

My runaway imagination,
Fed by the thundering boom,
Led to much speculation
Like Scrooge's dream of doom.

Were those figures on the wall
Just my own imagination?
Images that the mind recalls?
Pictures of my own creation?

Those shadows on the wall
Formed an eerie silhouette.
Something I should recall
Or something to forget?

Sleep did not come that night
To wipe away my reverie.
Watching shadows was my plight.
There was no sleep for me.

As the storm faded away,
Neath dawn's early light,
The start of a new day
Saw my candle still burning bright.

DREAM II

So many of my very good friends have passed away that I'm beginning to feel lonesome. At my age one must expect these things to happen but each time it does I feel a deep sense of loss and loneliness. Sometimes I dream of old friends and this poem is about those dreams. It is titled "Dream II" because of a previous poem entitled "Dream."

I dreamed of a long parade
Of all those I had known.
Those who had already made
That trip to the unknown.

Good friends through the years,
Close ties and fond memories.
Thought of them brings tears
And restless dreams like these.

I'd like to bring them back today
But well I know this cannot be.
I'll continue on my destined way
Till we are joined eternally.

DREAM III

Even though I can no longer see the stars at night my dreams often bring their images back to me. Along with memories of star-studded skies come dreams of my youth and the realization that I must not dwell too long in the past. This is my third poem about dreams, as indicated by the title.

A star-studded Georgia summer night,
Thoughts that drift on pale moonbeams.
Everything seems to be so very right,
Bringing back to me my youthful dreams.

Much of my dreaming is of the past,
Of wild youth, adventure and flight.
Good memories that will always last,
And get me through each long night.

Dreams of blasting off at night,
Jet flames trailing in my wake.
Such a bright and awesome sight,
Memories that time cannot take.

The flights through endless space
Into dark clouds and bright sky.
Aerobatics with all their grace,
Things that fearless youth try.

Now that I must no longer fly
Because of dim and failing sight
I sometimes wonder and ask why
That this should be my plight.

Dreams of the dim past give way,
To dreams of that which is new.
Dreams of a new and better day,
With so many new things to do.

This dreaming on a starry night
Brings on a new perspective
Of so many things that I might
Think of as a new objective.

Music, poetry and literature,
Much more fitting for my age.
Things that will all endure,
Until I turn life's last page.

DREAM IV

As you may have noticed, I dream quite often. Some of my dreams are pleasant and some are nightmares, but the subject has always intrigued me. Perhaps I need an interpreter to tell me what they mean, if anything.

My dreams can transport me
To places I have never seen.
And in this kind of fantasy,
I always "Make the scene."

I now can lead a double life,
Often in a different place.
Sometimes it is filled with strife,
Sometimes filled with grace.

Sometimes terror is my fate.
A nightmare full of strife,
In which dangers are so great
And I am fearful for my life.

Often I go to foreign lands
And talk with people there.
Then the world is in my hands
And I am free from care.

Who knows where next I'll be
In my dreamland of fantasy?
Who knows what next I'll see?
It's always a mystery to me.

NOSTALGIA

Remembering the past and wallowing in nostalgia can be fun, but often serves as a reminder of the passing years and the disturbing fact that you are getting older. Here are some poetic thoughts on the subject.

Do you remember those days of yore,
Those visits to the ten cent store,
Those good old golden days, when,
Each town had its five and ten?

The matinee at the picture show
Was the very best place to go,
For if you were feeling forlorn,
You could always have popcorn.

Shave and a haircut, two bits.
You were putting on the ritz,
When you could spend a quarter
For a shave with scented water.

Model T's were the latest thing
To make the cash registers ring.
They were very cheap, but shucks,
Who could raise six hundred bucks?

Then you worked for a whole day,
Making a dollar, darn good pay!
And it only cost one thin dime,
To have a rollicking good time.

The drugstore, a favorite stop;
A nickel would get you soda pop.
The druggist was an old, old friend
Who always kept you on the mend.

If you remember all these things,
That play upon your heart strings,
And you've survived all these years,
Escaping those Alzheimer's fears:

Then you have reached the time,
For your glorious second prime,
Now friends might be so bold,
As to say, "You're getting old."

ON REACHING EIGHTY

The aging process didn't seem to bother me until I reached eighty. Most things have been down hill since. I'm not complaining and I thank the Lord for each new day. This poem is just my way of letting off a little steam.

After passing the age of eighty
I know not what to anticipate
And wonder if, in coming years,
I will continue to disintegrate.

After passing the age of eighty
All sorts of problems began.
I never realized so many things
Could possibly happen to one man.

For me, reaching the age of eighty
Was one of life's crucial points.
For prior to that awesome birthday,
I was not aware of all my joints.

Stiffness gets to be a problem
When joints don't want to bend.
Doctors say that it's Arthritis
But can't tell us how to mend.

Putting on pants in the morning
Never seemed so very hard
Before that eightieth birthday.
Now my leg is like a solid rod.

To insert that unbending leg
I lean against a solid wall
And hope to get the other leg
Into my pants without a fall.

After passing the big eighty
I have now begun to find out
That there is another problem
Which is sometimes called Gout.

On the upper side of eighty
We have much steeper stairs
And it is now more difficult
To get up out of chairs.

When young I used to think
There was no need for glasses.
But now that I'm past eighty
I need them more as time passes.

Before the age of eighty
Walking was an easy feat.
Now that I'm past eighty
I have trouble with my feet.

Eighty years have come and gone
Not without some compensation.
There is a modicum of respect
For we of the older generation.

Now that I'm well past eighty,
In the so-called Golden Years,
I put my trust in almighty God,
Whose grace stills all my fears.

CELEBRATION

In the months before I turned eighty years old, I kept telling myself, "So far, so good." Since I have already beaten the odds concerning the life span of males in the United States, my thoughts sometimes turn to the subject of mortality. I imagine this is normal for anyone in this age bracket, especially when so many friends have already gone. I am hoping for an easy transition from this life to the next and see no reason to fear this rite of passage. I have tried to express my feelings on the subject in "Celebration."

Mourn not for my demise,
Let there be a celebration
For him whose sacrifice
Leads me to my destination.

As I near the end
Of life on planet earth,
I know I have a friend
To help with my rebirth.

His forgiveness of sin
Makes it possible for me
To find my way in
To wonders yet to be.

These wonders, yet to be,
May be my destination
And reason enough for me
To have a celebration.

TWILIGHT TIME

When younger I thought of persons in their eighties as being old, real old. Now that I have reached that plateau I realize that it's just another stage in life. President Reagan spoke of reaching his twilight years. That's one way of looking at it but I prefer to think of it as a challenge. Of course there are problems and new problems pop up, but that's life, isn't it? God willing, problems will be met and overcome. I have found that a good sense of humor always helps.

As I approach my twilight years,
I find that there are many fears,
Most of which I never had before.
Now they haunt me more and more.

For example, there's that little pot,
That won't remain in its allotted spot.
It slowly sinks below my middle,
And, to me, that's quite a riddle.

Why won't things remain in place,
And stay in their proper space?
I never thought a chin would cause trouble,
But now I look and see it is double.

The hair on top is getting thin,
And I do not know just when
The bald spot that's up there,
Will rid me of remaining hair.

And now, weight is a problem.
Pounds--wonder how I got 'em?
Never a problem in the past...
Now I'm on a constant fast.

Memory seems to come and go,
And right now I do not know,
How I'm ever going to find
This poem's end. It's slipped my mind.

THE AGING PROCESS

Have you been to a doctor with aches and pains only to have him tell you "It's just part of the aging process" or "You're doing fine for a person your age"?

A doctor tries to ease our mind,
And calm our mounting stress,
By telling us that he finds
"It's just the aging process."

This so-called aging process
Seems to happen to us all
And I must now confess
That I'm not thrilled at all.

It seems to be inevitable
And there isn't any way
To make it more acceptable
No matter what they say.

That impressive medical degree
The doctor earned in college
Does not help you and me.
What a waste of knowledge!

With dimming sight and hearing too
And possibly Arthritis,
I've lost my taste for daring-do
And now fear Gingivitis.

With bulges in wrong spaces
And clothing that's too tight,
Gaping in awkward places,
I suck it in with all my might.

I've even had a change in pace
And now walk a different way.
I once walked with ease and grace
But now I shuffle and I sway.

Memory comes and goes
Like a pendulum that swings
And added to my woes,
I've trouble finding things.

These problems accumulate
Into one total mess.
Oh, what an awful fate
Is this AGING PROCESS.

STARS

I remember as a youth, on lazy summer evenings, looking up at the night sky and marveling at the enormity of the universe. I imagine everyone has pondered over what happens after death. Every time I look up at the stars I wonder if they might be the home for our souls.

Give not the stars that shine
Nor the sun and moon to me,
For they are already mine…
A gift of grace, you see.

No matter what the days bring
Or what my future be
My soul will always sing
Throughout eternity.

And if my soul comes to rest
On some far distant star
I will do my very best
To remember you from afar.

Stars that twinkle so bright
In our far flung galaxy
May make you wonder some night
If one of them is home for me.

SIREN IN THE NIGHT

Often, in the night, while watching TV or working on a poem, I hear a siren in the distance. As it approaches my location, the sound increases in volume until it reaches a loud crescendo, then begins to fade in the distance. I remember reading some technical articles about audio, radar and sonar in which this was described as the Doppler effect. The sound of those sirens in the night always give me an uneasy feeling. A feeling that someone is in trouble and in need of help and why am I not doing something about it. Then comes the realization that the sound of those sirens means that help is on the way. Here are some of my thoughts in poetic form.

A siren in the night,
Symbol of someone's plight.
The peace of night shattered,
As if nothing else mattered.

The sound starts from afar
Soon arriving with a jar
That reaches a tirade
Before it begins to fade.

This eerie Doppler effect
Is often able to direct
My thoughts to wonderings
About unpleasant things.

What does that siren sound imply?
Is someone about to die?
Or is this siren on it's way
To rescue someone where they lay?

I sometimes have the fear
That the last sound I will hear
Just possibly might be
A siren in the night for me.

AS TIME GOES BY

As I grow older the passage of time seems to accelerate. I do not know much about the theory of relativity but I do know that one's concept of time is relative. It depends on your point of view and how you use what time you have.

Time can be a relative thing,
Fall may seem longer than spring.
In youth time seems to creep,
Yet in age time seems to leap.

Remember those long days in school
When being on time was the rule?
While sitting through each long class
You thought the time would never pass.

Recesses were of another sort,
They were always far too short.
Vacations never seemed to last,
They were gone all too fast.

In middle age time seems to float.
With age we all begin to note
That time seems to accelerate
As we pass each new birth date.

Then, as we turn another page,
And reach that "Golden Age"
When time seems to race
At quite a faster pace

Our concept of time's passage
May depend upon time's ravage.
But experience will surely bring
Knowledge of time's relative thing.

THE ESSENCE OF TIME

"Time is of the essence." How often have you heard that phrase used to emphasize the need for haste? There are many other aspects of time and, to me, the most important is that we only have so much of it.

Time is of the essence,
So I have been told,
And I do believe it
Since I am growing old.

I have also been told
That time is a relative thing
And this too I believe
Since I have felt its sting.

I have reached that certain age
Of realization, with astonishment,
That I have reached life's stage
Of diminishing accomplishment.

There is never enough time
To get everything done.
Each new job is more important
Than the previous one.

Then there are priorities.
How do you apply the test
To find which pending task
Is more important than the rest?

Time is a valuable commodity.
We should cherish every bit
Because the essence of time
Is the way one uses it.

RELATIVE TIME

The older I get the faster time passes. After discussing this with friends my age, I have concluded that this is just another part of the aging process, When I was young I had time for everything. Now, that I'm older, there is never enough time to do all the things I want to do. Time must be a relative thing.

They say that time is relative
And I believe "they" are right,
Because in these "Golden Years"
Time seems rapid in its flight.

In youth time seems forever,
There is no end in view.
In old age time is precious,
With remaining days too few.

Years slip by so very fast.
A month seems like a week,
Weeks pass just like days,
And days are just a streak.

Why does the aging process
Appear to make time fly?
Years, so long in youth,
Now seem to just fly by.

Perhaps it all balances out.
Youth is given time to sow
The seeds of all the wisdom
That it later needs to know.

MEMORY

The aging process, which was the subject of one of my previous poems, seems to bring about many little irritating things. One of those irritations appears to be lapses of memory concerning recent events. Memories of the distant past are easily recalled but current events often slip away before we know it. Now, don't tell me that I'm headed for Alzheimer's disease. I know too many perfectly normal people with this problem. Anyway, I am waiting for the time when my brain can be fitted with a new pentium processor to bring me right up to date. Today's poem has to do with my little irritating memory problems.

My memory seems to come and go,
And now what I would like to know
Is just what it is that I should do.
When I'm not—I think I'm through.

When I start to set the clock
And hear the front door knock,
I hurriedly answer the door
And clock memory is no more.

Then the clock chimes the hour
And memory that had gone sour
Returns with a quick reminder
That the clock needs a winder.

Sometimes at the refrigerator
I wonder what I came there for.
The memory of what I desired
Seems to have quickly expired.

My memory sometimes slips a cog
And then it needs a gentle jog
Just to straighten all things out.
Now what is it that this poem's about?

IN THE MIDDLE OF THE NIGHT

This poem is dedicated to my wife, Hattie Mina. After fifty five years of marriage she is still my sweetheart and comforter. Of course we have our ups and downs but at the end of every day all is forgiven and all's right with the world.

When each day is through,
I long to be with you,
And want to hold you tight
In the middle of the night.

In the middle of the night,
Waking from nightmare's fright,
I feel the warmth of you
And know the dream's not true.

In the middle of the night,
When I often wake with pain,
I can simply hold you tight,
Knowing life is not in vain.

When anxieties accumulate,
And I worry about my fate,
You make everything alright,
In the middle of the night.

And when the night has ended,
It is you on whom I've depended
To make everything just right
In the middle of the night.

A LADY'S SHOES

Often when waiting for my wife to get dressed I wonder what takes so long. When she finally shows up it usually turns out that selecting just the right pair of shoes to go with the outfit she is wearing caused the delay. That plus listening to conversations with friends concerning shoes and a few glimpses into her closet led to this poem.

What is it with women and their shoes?
They never seem to have the desired pair.
Even though the shoe closet is loaded,
The looked for color is never there.

Women's shoes come in many styles.
There are both low and high heels
With so very many colors and tints
That the hapless male mind reels.

This thing women have about shoes…
Could it be some kind of obsession?
There must always be the right pair
For each dress in their possession.

Each dress of any particular color
Must have a pair of shoes to match.
If the lady has a lot of dresses
Her shoes can become quite a batch.

A lady's closet may be overflowing
With dresses and shoes of every kind
Yet "she doesn't have a thing to wear."
It's enough to blow the poor male mind.

TALKING WOMEN

The idea for this poem rattled around in my mind for quite a while. With my sight as it is I often have to follow my wife to get around. As she stops to talk with her women friends I become a silent partner. Their conversations are continuous streams of talk, and even if I had something to add, I would have difficulty getting a word in edgewise.

I never could quite understand
How women can keep on talking.
It must not be something planned,
But comes natural, like walking.

Let a few women get together
And talking starts right away,
Just as if there were never, ever
Going to be another day.

If some hapless male be present,
He would probably fail to realize
That talking women might resent
His getting a word in edgewise.

Hence it's my advice to men
That if you know what's best
Never ever try to break in
Upon any women's talk fest.

STRONG WOMEN AND MACHO MEN

It is said that women live longer than men. This could eventually lead to women controlling most of the nation's wealth. Who knows, we might be in better economic shape.

I once thought men were strong
And women the weaker gender.
It did not take me very long
To see man is just a contender.

Can men bear the pain of birth?
I doubt that any man would trade
With any woman on this earth
If arrangements could be made.

Statistically women live longer
By some eight years I'm told.
Perhaps they are the stronger
And they may be just as bold.

These modern times make it clear,
Women are active in every field.
Men must face their worst fear
And now be prepared to yield.

Men no longer lead the way.
Women may now be astronauts.
Macho men no longer hold sway
Over deeds as well as thoughts.

Strong women may be contrary,
Their whims may be pretended,
Therefore men must be wary
And their machismo defended.

Will unisex be the final end
When no distinctions are made?
Will gender be a perfect blend
And men's machismo finally fade?

Men's machismo may be fading
Into some never never land,
While the women are parading
Their strength on every hand.

Who knows what might have been
Had Eve behaved back then?
But here's to strong women
And here's to macho men.

THE DOCTOR'S WAITING ROOM

Have you ever wondered why there is so much waiting in a doctor's waiting room? I know that emergencies can wreck office schedules but I do think there could be more efficient scheduling. On one of my visits to the doctor I had plenty of time and agonized waiting to outline this poem.

While in the doctor's waiting room,
My thoughts turn to impending doom.
So uncomfortable and ill at ease,
Have you had thoughts like these?

My appointment was for ten a.m.
By now I'm thinking of mayhem.
My lunch time has crept past,
How long will this waiting last?

The magazines were all passe.
Newspapers were from yesterday.
No matter how hard I tried
Nothing could keep me occupied.

The room was either too cold or hot
And a draft was blowing at my spot.
Were all these people watching me?
Their furtive glances seemed to be.

My name was finally called out.
It sounded like a loud shout.
I slowly rose from my chair
Stiff from long sitting there.

At last the waiting was no more.
As I entered the patient's door,
Those feelings of impending doom
Accompanied me into that room.

The diagnosis was not so bad.
Thoughts of doom that I had
Were just useless trepidation
Without any real foundation.

I should have learned right here
About controlling unfounded fear.
But still the doctor's waiting room
Brings me thoughts of impending doom.

SOUNDS IN THE NIGHT

My wife, Hattie Mina, has never let me forget, nor has she forgiven me for letting her get up in the night to take care of the children while I slept. She could never understand how I could sleep through the sounds of our children, yet be instantly awakened by the slightest mechanical noise.

During our child raising years
I flew many a different plane.
The events of those past days,
In my memory will always remain.

When piloting an aircraft
Certain sounds are germane
To the operation and safety
Of that particular plane.

At home, in bed, late at night,
Almost any mechanical sound
Would bring me bolt upright.
My wife's reaction was profound.

If the air conditioner fan
Slowed down or speeded up,
I would hear that difference,
Wake, and ask her, "What is up?"

Her memory of those past days
Is somewhat more introspective.
As a mother, she was the best...
Of her children, most protective.

She was quick to take action
If a child cried in the night.
But the sounds the child made
Had nothing to do with flight.

So I slept peacefully serene
When the children cried out.
But at any mechanical noise,
I was quickly up and about.

This seemed reasonable to me
Since I was trained that way
But my wife has never understood
Even to this very day.

She has not yet forgiven me
For ignoring children's cries,
While immediately reacting to
Mechanical sounds of the skies.

SOLILOQUY AT DAWN

Getting out of bed in the morning is sometimes a problem for me. I usually wake up around five A.M. and that is when poems come to mind. Maybe I'm a morning person. At any rate the decision to get up is often defeated by "A Soliloquy At Dawn."

As each new day dawns
With a glimmer of light,
I wonder if it warns
Me of my sorry plight.

Limitless possibilities,
Adventures will unfold,
And what new businesses
Does this new day hold?

With much anticipation
And thoughts very bold,
Comes the realization
That I am getting old.

With this revelation
Of harsh reality,
My eager anticipation
Turns to lethargy.

My usual early walk
Seems much less exciting.
At exercise I balk,
The bed is more inviting.

To rise or not to rise,
That was my vexation.
It came as no surprise,
That I chose relaxation.

MY CLONE

The subject of cloning has been much discussed in the news lately, raising some interesting and bothersome questions. Of course cloning has been a regular procedure in botany for a long time. Now that scientists have cloned animals, the natural question is "Where do we go from here?" I do not pretend to have an answer but hope that research in this field might lead to elimination of disease. It seems to me that human nature has a built-in clone and that leads to this poem.

If the truth were known
I might be a clone.
Somehow I always knew
That I was really two.

One of me is always glad
The other one is always sad.
No matter what I do
There's another point of view.

My clone does not agree,
On things that we see.
To me, a tree's a tree.
To him, it might not be.

My decisions are often split,
My clone doesn't want to sit
On my side of the fence
Without some recompense.

No matter what I do
My clone is there too,
Demanding his point of view
Be part of my review.

It would be very nice
Not to always think twice.
Have thoughts, my very own,
No interference from that clone.

THE PSYCHE

I have always been a science fiction fan. Many years ago I saw a science fiction movie that left a lasting impression with me. The title was The Forbidden Planet. The thing that impressed me most was the plot handling of the Id. The planet's inhabitants had been wiped out but the collective Id of the total population had survived as psychic energy. Of course the plot had many other complications but the subject of the Id always facinated me. As my grandmother used to say "it's mind boggling" and it still is. Here are my most recent thoughts on the subject.

The Psyche, the Id and the Ego;
Have you ever wanted to know
Why you act the way you do?
Psychoanalysts say they always knew.

After searching through large tomes,
I am amazed at how the mind roams.
Psyche, Id and Ego are all defined
As functions of the soul and mind.

Psyche is the mind as an entity,
Id the source of psychic energy,
Ego governs the mind's action rationally.
All of which leaves me close to insanity.

My Psyche, Id and Ego have concluded
That these thoughts have intruded
Upon my peace, calm and serenity
And could, perhaps, affect my sanity.

So I have told my Psyche, Id and Ego
Just where I think that they should go
And leave me with my serenity
And also with my equanimity.

OLD SOUTHERN CUSTOMS

Old southern customs are fading and changes are taking place today. It seems to me that some changes could be made to our advantage. With modern day technology most anything is possible.

How often have you heard the phrase:
"It's an old southern custom?"
Now in these modern days,
The phrase is a conundrum.

In days long past we southerners
Could choose our way of living.
And if we had our druthers,
We would do a lot of sitting.

Modern ways have changed all that,
Our southern drawl is fading.
Instead of a friendly chat,
We now all have call waiting.

No longer do we slowly say:
"So long cuzzen, yawl come back"
Now in this modern day
That would be off track.

Remember, if you can,
Those golden days of yore,
When a southern gentleman
Could never be a bore.

He always tipped his hat
To ladies he would meet.
He always stood and never sat
When he could offer them a seat.

His manners were impeccable,
His ladies were respectable,
His ancestors were traceable,
And he was quite reliable.

Those were old southern customs,
A more slow and easy way.
They were not in the doldrums
But just a more genteel way.

With technology here to stay,
Androids may be with us soon.
If programmed the southern way
They could become a boon.

What a future this could be,
Filled with charm and grace,
With old southern hospitality
In each and every place.

Robots trained this genteel way
Would be a charming custom.
If greeting guests, they could say,
"It's an old southern custom."

SEASONS

As I take my walks, during the beautiful autumn season, and see how the good earth perpetuates itself with the changing seasons, I often wish that we humans could do the same. Here are some further thoughts on this subject.

As the seasons come and go,
Autumn is a beautiful time of year.
Leaves are turning everywhere,
And Thanksgiving is drawing near.

Squirrels storing nuts for winter,
Birds flying south ere it's too late,
Hardy fall flowers in full bloom,
As nature prepares to hibernate.

A little nip is in the air,
And frost is on its way
To color autumn leaves,
In such a beautiful way.

The life span of we humans
As compared to nature's plan,
Is made up of four seasons,
During the normal life span.

Now that I'm in my autumn days,
I wonder what winter will bring.
Considering the seasons of my life,
I long for the return of spring.

A WINTER DAY

As I was walking one cold, damp, wintry morning, my spirits were as dreary as the weather. My thoughts were on things I had not done and problems that needed solving. Suddenly the clouds were blown away and the sun drenched everything with bright warm sunlight. My thoughts and my disposition changed with the clearing sky and today's poem is the result.

The sun hides behind a cloudy sky,
This winter day is cold and dreary.
I'm sure that it's the reason why,
It's hard for me to feel cheery.

I know the sun is still up there,
And that tomorrow is another day,
But like the sky, my soul is bare,
And I'm not ready for another day.

It seems I've forgotten to remember
There's nothing so certain as change,
And as sure as fall follows September,
This weather is going to change.

A warm wind scatters the overcast.
The radiant sun again shines bright.
The dreary winter day has passed,
And this day is filled with sunlight.

Sunlight to make me realize
That every day can be as bright,
If I would only visualize
Each day drenched in sunlight.

MY FAVORITE TIME OF DAY

I became accustomed to getting up early during thirty years in the military. Quite often I was required to make pre-dawn flights. Being a fighter pilot I was always alone in my plane and witnessed some beautiful dawns. I guess my early morning walks are as close as I can get to those memories. That time of day is still my favorite.

My favorite time of every day
Is in the morning, six to nine,
When I take my walks alone
And call those moments mine.

I get to see the dawn break
And hear the world come alive.
It is a thrill to see
Each new day arrive.

The sun peeks over the horizon
With the pink blush of dawn.
Morning traffic starts to build
And late risers begin to yawn.

Traffic builds to a deafening roar
As toilers hurry to their work.
You'd think there was a race,
In which drivers went berserk.

By now it's nearly nine o'clock,
The magic morning does not last.
The day's routine has now begun,
And my favorite time has passed.

DAWN WALK

Usually, for at least five days each week, I walk two miles early in the morning. I try to start my walks at first light, just as dawn is breaking. This is a wonderful time of day with very little traffic and only the sounds of nature occasionally interrupted by a distant train whistle. A perfect time to collect your thoughts and plan for the coming day. In my case this often includes an idea for a poem. Here are my thoughts on one early spring morning.

On my early morning walks,
While a new day breaks,
It seems that nature talks
As the sleeping town awakes.

With dawn's first glimmer of light,
Just before the sun comes up,
A gentle breeze sweeps away the night
As if the Lord were cleaning up.

Tree frogs start their chirping
And birds begin to sing.
The whole world is singing
A salute to early spring.

The sun's golden ray
Slices through a tree
Announcing a new day
Perfectly made for me.

A DAY IS BORN

Dawn is my favorite time of day. This poem seemed to write itself as I walked the back streets of my home town enjoying the sunrise at daybreak.

Streets without their usual throngs,
Amber street lights still glowing,
Tree frogs rasping out their songs,
The first light of dawn is showing.

A brand new day is dawning
With a chance to start anew.
A grand bright new morning
Made fresh with early dew.

Song birds beginning their ritual.
New buds eagerly awaiting the sun.
There must be something spiritual
As each glorious new day is begun.

Then the sun's orange orb
Peeks above the earth's rim
And the sky seems to absorb
Light, and is no longer dim.

A glorious new day is born,
God's wonderful gift to man,
Who should, at each new dawn,
Be thankful for God's plan.

SUMMER ZEPHYR

Sometimes my summer morning walks start in warm, damp, oppressive air. Then, just as the sun begins to show over the horizon, a cool breeze sweeps the atmosphere clear and clean.

Early on a sultry summer morn,
Just as a brand new day is born,
Humidity near a hundred percent,
Relief, it seems, is heaven sent.

The sun's fiery orb appears,
Another sweltering day nears.
When, suddenly, out of nowhere,
A cool breeze clears the air.

This gentle zephyr, just at sunrise,
So very often, comes as a surprise
To whisk away the stale summer air
That had, overnight, gathered there.

Perhaps the creator of all things
Sends down Angels, with beating wings,
To generate that early morning breeze.
Thank God for blessings such as these.

SUNRISE SERENADE

In spring and summer, I try to get my morning walks in just before the sun comes up. The temperature is best, the traffic is less, the sun does not get in my eyes and I can listen to the talk shows and morning news on my pocket radio. There is another big advantage to walking at sunrise: the serenade from all the birds.

At the first rays of dawn's light
All the birds begin their chatter,
Singing with all their main and might
As though nothing else could matter.

Their songs fill the morning air
Blending into a mighty rhapsody
To be heard in the dawn's light
Like a grand and great symphony.

The soft cooing of the turtle doves
Tends to form a rhythmic background
For this serenade from the birds,
Which seems to come from all around.

Occasionally one most audacious bird
Bursts forth with an outstanding aria
That overshadows all the rest
Of the songsters in the area.

He must be trying to impress
A female to become his mate.
From the volume of his song,
He really doesn't want to wait.

These lilting tunes fill the air
Each morning just at daybreak
And as I take my morning walk,
The songs seem just for my sake.

A FOGGY MORNING

My walks are often taken on fog shrouded mornings before sunrise. On these days there is a kind of eerie silence accompanying the fog, blanketing everything. As the rising sun wipes away the fog a beautiful day emerges.

Early morning ere the sun rises,
Before a brand new day begins,
Nature often brings surprises,
For the new day before it ends.

A misty morn with heavy dew,
Thick fog fills the sodden air
And stubbornly obstructs the view,
As calm and quiet is everywhere.

The sun slowly makes its way
Across the cloud covered sky.
An atmospheric change is underway,
Improvement in this day is nigh.

The sun soon burns away the fog.
Its warm rays of glorious light
Drive damp mists back to the bog,
Leaving the day clear and bright.

Sunbeams transform wet beads of dew
Into bright, shiny, glistening gems;
The foggy, misty morn now through,
The sun has solved its problems.

OL' YELLOW

Ol' Yellow followed me home
His tendency was to roam.
He would stop at every tree
Yet he continued to follow me.

He was a friendly cuss
Without pretension or fuss.
He wanted to be my friend,
I know not to what end.

I had no food to give
Nor place for him to live.
He asked no special favor,
Just wanted to be a neighbor.

Even though we could not talk
We communicated on that walk.
We did understand each other,
And he became my canine brother.

Such friends are hard to find,
There are few in human kind.
So now I look forward to see
Ol' Yellow waiting just for me.

THE TREE FROG'S SERENADE

For years I have been wearing hearing aids—the kind that fit into the ear canal and are not easily seen. My hearing loss is mostly in the high frequencies as a result of flying jet aircraft before we learned to protect ourselves from the jet engine noise. With these hearing aids certain frequencies are emphasized. It just happens that the noise made by tree frogs is exactly in that range.

During the midsummer heat,
When the air is still and clear,
I often hear a peculiar beat,
Coming from far and near.

At the beginning of each day,
And at every eventide,
Tree frogs come out to play,
Perhaps to seek a bride.

Although I've never seen one,
It seems they're everywhere,
Their raucous song is not done,
Till light or dark is there.

Tree frogs have their own sound.
Urrr-reee, (the sound heard by me).
It seems to come from all around
From each and every tree.

At times their rasping serenade
Becomes so loud it penetrates
Right through my hearing aid,
And in my brain it syncopates.

If these songs are amusing,
As their way to seek a mate,
I find it quite confusing,
As a way to seal your fate.

Urrr-reee, Urrr-reee, Urrr-reee,
Keeps blasting through my head.
Perhaps that's tree frogs' "Whoopee"
As they approach the nuptial bed.

WHAT MAKES THE MOCKINGBIRD SING?

For me, one of the first signs of spring is the sound of a mocking-bird. Its variety of songs seem to match the great variety of spring blossoms bursting forth everywhere. Each time I hear a mockingbird I wonder what prompted it to sing.

What makes the mockingbird sing?
Does he have his own agenda
Or is he just a harbinger of spring
With many songs to render?

Is he the master of his fate
Or are his lilting songs
His way of looking for a mate,
The one for whom he longs?

Does he mock all the rest,
Who sing with all their might,
Or does he want to be the best
Of all those who take flight?

I wonder if he ever dreams
Of a song he never heard.
A song with different themes
Than any other bird.

No matter what his motives are,
Or what his reasons be,
His glorious songs from afar
Are sweet music to me.

MISTY MORN

Early morning walks have been the inspiration for many of my poems. One spring morning, just before the sun came up, a misty haze brought visibility to near zero but when the sun came up everything changed to a beautiful day. This poem was published in The International Library Of Poetry's anthology for the year 2000.

A damp shroud covers the land,
As a pale light filters through.
A thick haze is all around,
To accompany the morning dew.

Quiet anticipation hovers in the air.
Even the birds are quiet this morn.
Everything in nature seems poised,
Waiting for a new day to be born.

Beams from the rising sun
Dissipate the damp haze,
Leaving a glorious morning,
One of God's best days.

Dew drops on a spider's web,
Shimmering in the sunlight
Like diamonds in a tiara,
Glistening so very bright.

The new day is beautiful,
God's blessings have been borne
On the shafts of sunlight
During this damp and misty morn.

FLOWERS AND US

Have you ever reflected on man's inhumanity to man? If you watch the daily news it would appear that there is no end to this inhumanity. I often watch the TV news before my morning walk and it is sometimes very upsetting. While I walk my agitation slowly subsides as I pass yards with beautiful flowers often accompanied by their faint aroma. This contrast between God's beautiful creations and how we humans, too often, live in it, led to this poem.

What a great and marvelous thing
Are flowers that bloom each spring;
A gift from heaven above,
An expression of God's love.

What an explosion of colors
Along with many sweet odors,
Like God's universal care,
His flowers are everywhere.

Flowers have never discriminated,
It's obvious, they are integrated.
Their colors mingle in every nation,
with never a sign of discrimination.

Wouldn't it be nice if we,
As human beings could agree,
That color does not decide
What's deep down inside?

In all of his creation
God made no stipulation
Regarding man or flowers,
As to their relative powers.

We are all God's creatures
Even though our features
Are never quite the same;
We know from whence we came.

OLEANDER

During my early morning walks many different aromas greet me along the way. The smell of bacon cooking, accompanied by many other morning cooking odors, gives me a hearty appetite by the time I get home. As I pass each yard the scent of flowers is often in the air. Each new aroma brings a memory or thought to mind. On one of these walks the scent of oleander blossoms led to thoughts about this particular plant and its blossoms.

While walking one cool misty morn
All kinds of scents were airborne
Including sweet flowering oleander.
That made my idle thoughts meander.

Pretty oleander, you smell so nice.
Why is it that you turn to vice?
Just touch a blossom and you'll see
How very poisonous oleander can be.

Like so many things in life
That lead to misery and strife;
They, at first, seem so sweet,
Only to end in total defeat.

Just as temptation's siren call
Will always lead to ethic's fall,
Oleander's scent does not explain
That to touch it leads to pain.

I guess there will always be,
A few oleanders for you and me,
Where sweet aromas may be found
Mid painful contacts all around.

IT'S IN THE BOOK

Some things I read and hear appall me. I wonder how the morals and ethics of this generation will affect coming generations. We seem to be departing from the intentions of this nation's founding fathers. We do have a book of instructions and a perfect example to follow.

My mind cries out for answers
Not knowing the questions to ask
Concerning my soul's assignment
During it's short earthly task.

I know there is a guidebook
With instructions for the trip.
But it seems that today's society
Doesn't think it's really "hip."

The book contains instructions,
with detailed command directions,
But this modern day civilization
Sees commandments as suggestions.

In today's modern muddled concept
Of what is right and what is wrong
It is sometimes so very convenient,
And much easier, to just go along.

In my search for the answers
I know just where to look.
When I need the right answer
I know IT'S IN THE BOOK.

THREE LITTLE WORDS

I have always been interested in semantics and in my experience have found that simple, little words can convey meanings best. Why use a long complicated, hard to understand word, if a short simple word will do? For example, I just followed my own advice. At the end of the previous sentence I used the word "do" instead of "suffice." In thinking along these lines, it occurred to me that there are three simple words that can make life much more pleasant. Hence this poem.

Three little words—"I love you,"
What a difference they can make
If these words are really true.
So use them for goodness sake.

Don't hesitate to use these words,
They are so easy to pronounce.
Be like the little song birds
Joyous love, eager to announce.

How many times in the past
Might problems have been solved,
And friendships made to last,
Were these three words involved?

No matter what the circumstance,
These words can pave the way
And give you a better chance
To bring about a better day.

Use these words in all sincerity,
And three more words, so very true,
Will appear in certain clarity,
And they are—"God loves you."

DAILY MIRACLES

Have you ever thought about the miracles that surround us every day? I know that I always accepted these wonderful gifts as just every day occurrences until I took the time to think about the wonderful miracles that continue to happen, every day.

Miracles happen each and every day,
They usually occur in such a way,
That we never seem to realize,
What is happening before our eyes.

The sun never fails to rise;
A miracle of considerable size.
The moon is there each night;
Another miracle for our sight.

The seasons continue to change,
And no one thinks, it strange.
Summer, fall, winter and spring
Continue to do their thing.

The miracle of life itself,
And the gift of good health,
Are marvels beyond compare,
Wonders we just know are there.

So many miracles every day,
Have left us quite blasé.
We accept them without thought
As to how they were wrought.

God, the creator of all things
Is the only one who brings
Miracles to us every day,
In his own inimitable way.

DENOMINATIONS

I keep hearing about the many various denominations within the Christian religion. I read about the split in some denominations bringing about, I suppose, another new denomination. It seems to me, that with only one guide book and one perfect example to follow, we Christians could reach an agreement.

Why so many denominations?
Was not Christ's teaching
Meant for all the nations?
Isn't that what we are seeking?

I wince when I am named
The member of some denomination.
Why couldn't we have remained
One world wide congregation?

Methodist, Baptist and Catholic too,
Presbyterian, Adventist and Episcopal
And that's just to name a few,
Too long a list to name them all.

Is this some kind of competition
To see who has the best rendition
Or who the better translation
Of God's sacred information?

I hope that when I die,
If anyone asks of my religion,
There is a quick reply:
"Why he was just a Christian."

ANTEBELLUM DAZE

When asked to do a poem for the hometown follies, concerning antebellum days, I was at a loss for words. It finally came to me that a southern gentleman from those days would have a hard time adjusting to today's society and vice versa.

If couples from days of yore
Could pass through time's door
They would be amazed to see
What has happened to society..

Those golden olden antebellum mores
Have been replaced by modern ways.
But there's one thing to never fail,
A woman's wiles will still prevail.

Those days were most exciting
And the women more enticing.
A true lady, never did reveal
The extent of her sex appeal.

A lady's antebellum dress
Let a gentleman only guess
At what would greet his sight
Upon their wedding night.

A man had only his imagination
To build up his anticipation
About the mysteries of life
To be revealed by his wife.

Today is a very different setting.
A man knows exactly what he's getting
Since all has been revealed to him
When modern ladies dress to swim.

Those golden olden antebellum days
Have been replaced by modern ways.
Perhaps because those antebellum mores
Would leave modern men in quite a daze.

THE MUSE AND I

The word "Muse" is French, stemming from the Latin Musa and the Greek mousa. In ancient Greek mythology there were nine muses of the arts, poetry and the sciences. They were the daughters of Zeus, the chief God, and Mnemosyne, the goddess of memory. Three of the muses were devoted to poetry: Calliope, the muse of epic poetry, Erato, the muse of love poetry, and Euterpe, the muse of lyric poetry. Today the word muse is used regarding the source of inspiration for poets, artists and scientists.

I often look for the muses
When I do my daily walk.
I have found better uses
For my time than idle talk.

Therefore I often walk alone
To enjoy my solitude,
And find that I am prone
All others to exclude.

Have I become a loner,
Without a single friend?
Victim of my own persona?
Oh what an awful end!

Thank God this is not true.
For poetry brings to me
Poetry readers just like you.
Newfound friends, yet to be.

And now, as I walk alone
With only the muse as company
I find that I have always known
My very best friend is poetry.

MORE

One morning while taking my walk and listening to a talk show on WYTH, Madison's radio station, the subject of greed was discussed. That inspired this poem which was just about completed, in my mind, during the walk. I rushed home to get it down on paper and I thank WYTH for the idea.

Adam and Eve had everything
And yet they wanted more.
It must be an inborn trait
We humans can't ignore.

No matter the circumstance
We just can't get enough.
And if we don't get more
We think it's really tough.

We always seem to think
That we are quite needy
But to tell the truth,
Most of us are greedy.

I wonder what it takes
To satisfy our desires.
Can that really happen,
Before one expires?

When we take the final step
On reaching Heaven's door,
Will we ask Saint Peter:
"Isn't there anything more?"

WALKING TALL

My wife came from the doctor's office one day and told me that she had lost several inches in height. To my amazement I found that I had suffered the same fate. My doctor said it was just part of the aging process. That didn't make me feel any better.

Can nothing be depended upon?
I thought my height was stable.
Now, to my surprise, I find
That's just another fable.

I know that buildings settle
And clothing does often shrink.
But to find that I shrink too
Does give me cause to think.

I have learned, that with age,
The cartilage in our joints
Dries up and shrinks away
At all the critical points.

After many years of this
There is a loss of altitude
Which may often bring about
A serious change in attitude.

An inferior complex can result
From looking up at your peers
Who are getting much taller
In these more recent years.

So, to improve my disposition,
When someone asks, "How yawl"
I stretch to my full height
And say "I'm walking tall."

THE LUSTER OF BRASS

Our son Stratton, his wife, Bonnie, and our granddaughters,
Morgan and Dana were visiting us for Christmas. We use the old Stokes-
McHenry house for guests and have them stay there during their visits.
My wife, Hattie Mina, started the mad rush to get everything just right
for them. One part of this ritual involves polishing the brass and silver.
It fell my lot to polish brass. I never realized that there is so much brass
in an old house. Andirons, fire screens, candelabra, lamps and all sorts
of things. During my hours of labor I developed a new appreciation for
highly polished brass.

The luster of polished brass
Is a fascinating thing to me.
Its depths reflect much more
Than the naked eye can see.

From below its surface sheen,
It reflects a deep golden light,
A dancing, gleaming golden glow,
That affects everything in sight.

This alloy of copper and zinc
Holds mysteries from the past.
The story of its discovery,
And the time it was first cast.

Did Cleopatra first see her face
In a mirror of polished brass?
For mirrors in the ancient world
Were only for the ruling class.

Did Leda and Helen of Troy,
Have mirrors of polished brass
To help them with their beauty,
Which affected men en masse?

Perhaps the catacombs of Rome
Were lit by flickering light
From candles in brass reflectors
To illuminate that eerie sight.

And now with every golden sunset
As another day is about to pass,
My thoughts and imagination turn to
The luster of highly polished brass.

SIGHT FLIGHT

Glaucoma ended my career as a fighter pilot and has continued to reduce vision as I grow older. I am now legally blind. Poetry and music have sustained me but I sorely miss flying as a pilot.

There are no vistas left for me,
No winding trails to distant sky
No sandy beaches by the sea,
No mountain passes still to try.
There are no vistas left for me.

A misty haze is all I see,
With murky figures passing by.
No recognition comes from me.
Could they know the reason why
There are no vistas left for me?

I miss those vistas in the air,
Ever present in my flight
With billowing clouds, oh so fair,
And endless twinkling stars at night,
But now there are no vistas left for me.

With vision dim and vistas past,
A wise voice within me says:
"Visions in your mind will last
For all of your remaining days,"
Yet no sighted vistas are left for me.

But God's grace is always there
And in my mind I can still see
His glorious creation everywhere.
No sighted vistas left for me,
But now a vision of eternity.

A FORMER PILOT'S PRAYER

Every time I hear a jet flying high overhead, memories of flying in the Air Force flood my mind. Those memories of flying jet fighters will always be with me.

My world was once a wondrous place
With unfettered realms of space.
I flew among the clouds up high
Jetting through windows in the sky.

I broke the barrier of sound
And in doing so I found
That nothing can compare
With that freedom in the air.

I knew the thrill of being free
Above the earth where one can see
Weather patterns as they form,
Forecasts of a coming storm.

All alone above the earth,
With a feeling of rebirth
That brings on a sensation
Of great power and elation.

The freedom that is only found
By those no longer earthly bound.
Free to soar into the sky
Loosing earthly bonds that tie.

Now those earthly bonds hold me
Because I can no longer see
To soar aloft on airborne wings
And listen to the wind that sings.

My world is now a smaller place.
I pray that God will give me grace
To accept the fact that I
May no longer soar the sky.

SUNSET

In addition to morning walks I often walk in the late afternoon and experience the sunset. I can only see some of the beautiful colors in the sunset sky, but can use memory, imagination and the perceptive feelings that accompany the sunset experience. I have tried to describe some of these perceptions in this poem.

That fiery orb of the sun sinks
Towards the edge of earth's rim.
Shadows stretch to great lengths
And daylight slowly starts to dim.

Color fills the western sky
Just as if some artist saint
Spread his palette, in a try
To match nature with his paint.

Another day comes to an end.
Darkness creeps over the land,
Creating a twilight blend,
From mother nature's hand.

Evening sounds now fill the air,
Replacing the day's noisy chatter.
It's time to forget all care,
And dream of things that matter.

As the gentle mantle of night
Spreads like a gossamer net
Over all that had been bright,
The sun has finally set.

DAY'S END

It seems that the muse of poetry descends upon me most often while I am taking my daily walk. Some of my walks are taken just before sunrise to avoid traffic. At other times I walk just as the sun is setting. On one of my recent sunset walks I became keenly aware of the transition from day to night and the accompanying sights and sounds. Of course this led to a poem.

Eventide, when shadows grow long,
And birds burst forth in song,
Little children come out to play.
Oh, what a lovely time of day!

The sun sets as a fiery ball,
Responding to the new night's call.
Cool breezes are wafting by,
Descending from a clear blue sky.

Wings of night enfold the day,
Darkness begins to hold sway.
Little glimmers of light appear,
As dark of night draws near.

Daylight sounds slowly fade away,
Nighttime's symphony begins to play.
A tinkling piano in the distance,
Heard because of its insistence.

A dog is heard barking from far away,
Proclaiming that someone passed its way.
All of mother nature seems to poise
As night sounds replace the daylight noise.

The quiet of night has arrived,
Mother nature has again survived.
The dark velvet of night descends,
As yet another golden day ends.

COLONEL DAN HICKY

Col. Dan McHenry Hicky was born June 28, 1917, in Madison, Georgia. After graduating from Morgan County High School in 1934, he attended the Georgia Military College for one year before transferring to the University of Georgia, where he received a bachelors degree in business administration (with a minor in fine arts) in 1938.

As noted in the text, Col. Hicky enlisted in the Army Air Corps in 1940, and after the start of the U.S. involvement in World War II, flew 25 combat missions in a P47 Thunderbolt in the European theatre. A lifetime member of the Daedalions, an association of airplane pilots, he is also a member of Lambda Chi Alpha Fraternity, the Blind Veterans Association, the International Society of Poets, and the American Legion.

At the time of his retirement from military service, he was the Deputy Comptroller of the Air Defense Command in Colorado Springs, Colorado.

Since returning to his hometown of Madison, Georgia, in 1972, Col. Hicky has served as President of the Morgan County Historical Society, the Morgan County Chamber of Commerce, and the Boxwood Garden Club.

He and his wife, Hattie Mina Reid Hicky are the owners of the historic Stokes-McHenry House, which is, according to Col. Hicky, the only home in Madison that has been continually owned and inhabited by the original family. He is the sixth generation to own the home, which was built in 1822.